MW01074590

What's Left of Me

Poems by Mick Stern

All contents, namely poetry, cover art, drawings, and book design, are by the author.

Published by the author.

I would like to thank my friend Gerd Stern for introducing me to *brevitas*, a loosely organized group of New York-based poets who read and respond to each other's poems. I am grateful for their insight and advice.

"Stopping by Slums on a Snowy Evening" and "Back to the Box" appeared in *First Literary Review-East.*

Edited by Cindy Hochman ("100 Proof" Copyediting Services)

All Rights Reserved, 2017, by Mick Stern

ISBN #: 978-1-365-66489-2

In Memory of Amnon Kehati and Celeste Rufo

TABLE OF CONTENTS

CONVERSATION WITH AN ONION

I once asked an onion,
Who am I?
I could have asked some lentils
or a carrot, but I only had
an onion.
The onion said,
First, peel off
name age address
Put away
family country religion
Carefully remove
language
gender
race
Discard your body
your thoughts
your memories
I said,
But what's left of me?
The onion replied,
You are the tears of joy and pain
that dried on your mother's cheek
when you were born.

COUNTRY OF STONES

All day the old man waits for his pension
in an office filled with old men
Finally, his name is called
The clerk gives him a stone

A victim of crimes against women
pleads for justice
The judge awards her a stone

A young man who is interested in politics
disappears
Weeks later, his family receives a package
containing a stone

The newspapers say
that stones make a nutritious soup
when boiled with dried grass and thorns

A crowd collects in the town square.
The president speaks in an amplified voice.
The crowd edges forward.
Many are already reaching for the stones
that lie heavy in every pocket
and every heart.

ADULTS RUSH IN

The child watches, in a rapture of attention,
the sway of branches in the breeze.
He has no motive or intention.
He almost becomes what he sees.

But he is not allowed this transformation.
Adults rush in and crash his reverie.
They tell him to praise God for creation,
but the child would rather praise the tree.

IN THE ANDES

One morning
we drove through a tiny pueblo
and encountered
a single traffic light
but no cars,
only a Quechua woman
with a baby on her back,
walking faster than red,
but more slowly than green.

'NIGHT, LEONARD

On Tuesday, the election
caused a worldwide plunge of hope.
Leonard Cohen did not live to see it.
He had slipped out of his body
on Monday. Was it coincidence?
Maybe he felt it coming—
a new order that has no use for him
or anybody like him.
Maybe this new regime reminded him
of the old ones that murdered Lorca and Neruda
Maybe he just didn't like the idea
of living through a night
so long and dire that nobody knows
where the next dawn will come from.

November 2016

BACK TO THE BOX

I'm thinking inside the box again.
It's getting too crowded and noisy outside the box
Everyone is following the same signs:
"Exit Box—Left Lane Only"
They are all welcome to keep on going
and leave me to my square thoughts.

BAD INVESTMENT

I am a boomer, born midcentury
into a perfect traditional family.
Grew up in a subdivision
filled with other perfect traditional families.
Indeed, the only flaw in all this perfection
seemed to be me.
My father called me "Bad Investment"
because of my expensive dental work

and poor grades in math.
When I got tired of his disapproval,
I'd slip out of the house
and run and shriek with my friends
Joey, Timmy, Cathy, Denise, and Bob,
also known as Waste of Space,
Extra Mouth to Feed,
Does Dumb Things,
and What They Don't Tell You About Having Kids.

BALKAN LULLABY

Stumbling out of a tavern,
I reach into my pocket for matches
and find fingers that don't belong to me
busy removing coins
that don't belong to them.
Brother, help yourself.
Let's share a smoke.
Look, under these exhausted beech trees,
how deeply sleeps the baby.

At the urging of passionate accordions,
Grandfather dances his belly to the bar.
Don't ask him who plays cards
in the back room all night.
It's only a crime if the police don't get their cut.
Tell those drunks to stop yelling or
they'll wake the baby.

Across the border,
sun flashes on binoculars.
You can't cross the river here.
An army tore down the bridge
to prevent another army from doing it first.
We pile our belongings on a horse cart.
Our destination is any place where life goes on.
Frost sparkles in the grass.
Hush now, darling, calm down.
Let sleep close your tearful eyes.

THE NEW MARTYRS

The new martyrs will soon be as dead
as the old martyrs

Maybe deader

The new martyrs
scorn the doubts and the hesitations
of the old martyrs

The new martyrs have no patience
for long explanations
They yearn for the moment of truth
the final curtain
the last tango
the all-fall-down

Dying gives them something to live for
They don't even carry explosives
or wear suicide vests

They can blow themselves up
with their own rage

BREAKABLE

Naomi's third or fourth attempt to make a vase
was accidentally marvelous—an aquamarine
bowl with floating birds, waves in the sky,
and one crazy fish walking backwards.
We put it on the coffee table in the living room.
One day, Naomi's mother, who was old and unsteady,
fell on the coffee table. The bowl fell down
and shattered. Miraculously, she was unharmed.
She could have cracked her wrist, her hip, her head.
The floor was littered with shards.
It was more than an accident. It was a warning.
Everything we cherish becomes fragile.

SHOESTRING CIRCUS

I am the owner of a shoestring circus.
Our tent is pitched on the windy beach of
lost umbrellas.

We had a thrilling wireless act,
but a monkey unplugged the WiFi.
Now the acrobats perform without the Net.

Last week the clowns refused
to be shot out of cannons,
so we turned the cannons on them.
We're still sweeping up clown dust.

Our freak show features
brokers, bankers, politicians.
Don't get too close to their cages.
Their smiles are full of teeth.

Bad news at the box office.
Tattooed punks who used to work for me
now perform in the streets for small change.
Ticket sales are down, we need to cut costs.
Tomorrow the elephants go on a diet.

13

BUFFALO, AGO

One day, I will never go back.
I'll stop returning to memories
of a white frame house
and snowy streets
where I threw my yellow hat away
and told my mother I lost it.

While the family slumbered,
I leaned at my window
to watch distant trains passing,
the infinite boxcars of the Erie Lackawanna,
the train whistle breaking a long, empty hush.

I cherished my loneliness because it was mine.
Tried to keep it my secret,
but you knew beyond asking.
No questions or answers, only languid afternoons
filled with the drone of lawn mowers
and the buzzing of insects
whose life lasts a few summer hours.

By chance for each other
we were like medicine,
though medicine is bitter.
Furtively, gently, a few drops of affection
seeped all the way down
to the core of our youth

ACCORDING TO VLADIMIR

Vladimir and I are standing
in front of an auto body shop in Brooklyn
waiting for my car to be fixed.
Vladimir exhales a blue cloud
of cigarette smoke and says,

"God and the devil are the same thing.
Everything depends on the tension
between good and evil.
If only evil existed,
mankind would destroy itself in two weeks.
If only good existed,
the boredom of absolute perfection
would eventually make people
lose their will to live."

The mechanic comes out
wiping his hands with a rag. He says,
"Your car is ready. It's not perfect, but it runs."

BUENOS AIRES

is a lady well past her prime
but still lively and flirtatious.

She may greet you
with aristocratic disdain
or household warmth.

She spends her days in cafés
discussing philosophy and *fútbol,*
her nights in tango bars.

She's doesn't like harbor rats
or economists.

And that old, tattered dress she always wears?
In her mind it is still as glamorous
as the day that it arrived by boat from Paris
one hundred years ago

I HEAR VOICES

The war veteran who opened fire in an airport,
killing people at random, reportedly told police
that he heard voices urging violence.
He thought these voices were inside his head.
But they weren't.

WOMAN IN A BOX

Every morning she exchanges
the box she rents
for the box she works in.
All day long she stares at numbers
flickering on her screen.
Her box is surrounded
by other boxes—
rows of boxes, floors of boxes,
blocks of boxes. At dusk,
the city shuts down
like the lid of a blind eye,
but she continues
to watch the numbers
jump around her screen.
She doesn't want to lose her job
and end up living in
a cardboard box.

19

GOLGOTHA FOR YOUR TROUBLE

The thief nailed up
on the right side of Christ
said to the thief nailed on the left side,
"How come Jesus gets eternal glory
and we get nothing but pain?"
The thief on the left said,
"Yes, aren't we *all* sons of God?"
Christ said, "No, no, no,
you don't understand!"
A centurion shouted,
"Shut the fuck up!
I'm sick and tired of this endless blah-blah-blah
about whose god is the best.
That's one reason I hate Judea.
Another is the heat."

OPEN AIR FLEA MARKET

An invitation to mingle with unnecessary objects.
A stroll between piles of homeless artifacts.
A lesson in the surplus waste of consumerism.
The final resting place for souvenir ashtrays ,
Old West belt buckles and Confederate bedpans.
A jungle where "hunters"
collect and "gatherers" acquire.
A chance to buy items that are worth nothing.
A market where the buyer is clueless,
the seller is truthless, and the goods are useless.
The protected habitat of endangered things,
like tobacco pipes, pressure cookers, hula hoops,
cassette players, three-hole paper punchers,
cocktail shakers, Rolodexes, pin-up calendars.
A hospice for dying appliances.
A *Salon des Refusés* for paintings that nobody wants.
A dump for clothes that have never been in style
and never will be.

GETTING AWAY FROM IT ALL

Make sure that the children are in their cages
before we leave for the airport.

Kelly works for a non-profit organization that feeds
homeless cannibals.

During the self-esteem seminar, a drunken flounder
laminated on my sofa.

Due to an outbreak of equine flu, people stopped eating
horseradish.

How many words is Wordsworth worth if Wordsworth is
worth words?

SIGNIFICANCE

Vampires battle Zombies in Galaxy 27.

Two young people fall in love while searching for the perfect muffin.

Girl must choose between high school sweetheart and college boyfriend.

Every semester I tell my screenwriting students
that their story ideas are not very deep.
I point out, as gently as possible,
that their stories lack significance.
A girl waves an eager hand.
"Professor, what do you mean by *significance?*"
I take a deep breath and say,
"The things that we care about, like birth, death, money,
power, love, family, work, courage, betrayal,
freedom, illness, war, injustice..."
As I speak she scribbles furiously
this handy little list of what makes life so important.

THE SWEETHEART EQUATION

"Honey, would you be a sweetheart and get me
a pillow
a magazine
a glass of water
a dish of cheese and crackers
a napkin to wipe my fingers
a cup of coffee
a crossword puzzle
a pencil with an eraser."

With each request
I become more of a sweetheart
and she becomes less.

FEAR OF ARCHITECTURE

Vaulted ceilings, skyscrapers,
looming towers, giant arenas, bridges
suspended over glittering water—
they make me nervous.
On wide marble stairs I feel insecurely footed.
In great halls I am belittled by vastness.
Majestic pillars and arches unbalance me;
so does an echoing dome.
I'd rather stroll through shady stone alleys
where time embraces decay,
where the family wash dangles from balconies,
and windows frame living faces.

THE ART OF CUTTING PAPER

For Béatrice Coron

The artist picks up a roll of dark paper
and unrolls it across her wide table
like the shadow of a tall building
lengthening at dusk.
From her studio she can see
Manhattan windows lighting up.
She cuts rows of little rectangles in the paper
filled with intricate silhouettes
that depict ordinary people
doing everyday things, like
dancing in their sleep,
fishing from their fire escapes,
flying over skyscrapers with mermaids.
Sometimes she has to put the blade down
and scroll through an Inbox
full of requests, deadlines, schedules.
Things that have to be done so she can
continue to do her real work,
which is cutting through surfaces
to release the light from the other side.

A SWIMMING POOL IN THE SAHARA

We drove south from clamorous Marrakesh,
half-blinded by dust and glare.
Had to stop for a herd of sheep in the road.
The shepherd wore a frayed *djellaba*
and leaned against the last fragment of an old wall,
the only shade for miles.

In a small town we saw a painted sign
for a hotel with a swimming pool—
A swimming pool in the Sahara!

But the water was warm and slimy
and dotted with insects. Later,
my wife spoke to the desk clerk.
"The pool is not what we had hoped for."
He murmured apologetically, then said,
"Hope always breaks its promises.
It is just a mirage.
We do not hope,
we only pray."

ACCIDENTAL

J.S. Bach left early in the morning.
His wife was upstairs having children.
He packed up his scales, left a note on the table,
and went to the church for rehearsal.
When he realized that the note was missing,
he he sent a choirboy to his house to fetch it.
When the boy returned to the church,
he stumbled and dropped the note.
It hit the old stone floor
with a loud echoing clangor
The choir applauded and laughed,
but just for a moment.
Bach's frown was like an early frost.
"Quiet, please! I am trying
to remain well-tempered."
But he was vexed because
the note was so disruptive.
He couldn't trust it
in a cantata or a motet.
He was the *Kappelmeister* of Leipzig
and the world's greatest composer,
but that note didn't give a damn.

SHE TOOK IT OUT OF MY HANDS

Waking to another day of gainful
but painful employment,
I decided to cancel my obligations,
so I pulled a pillow over my head.
But she took it out of my hands.
I got up, drank coffee, and picked up a book,
but she took it out of my hands
and urged me into rain and traffic.
All day I felt heavy, as if I carried a weight.
I didn't know where it came from
or what to do with it,
but when I got home,
she took it out of my hands.
We were sitting in a small room.
She made a smaller room for me with her arms,
and all that was heavy turned light.

THE POP-UP ARTIST
For Kyle Olmon

What kind of person
has the patience to spend years
assembling and disassembling
pop-up pages,
and the coldness necessary
to force them to reveal
their fragile magic?

He must be a perfectionist,
but not an extremist.
He must have
the mind of an engineer,
the eye of an artist,
the imagination of a child.

He must be mad
but methodical.

He is an architect of surprises.
He hides three dimensions inside two

and then dares you to turn the page.

DRIFTER

For Enrique Martínez

There is only one way to escape.
Leave at night.
Don't say goodbye to the people you love.
Amble in no particular direction
until you reach the Sargasso Sea,
but don't stop there.
Catch the next boat out
and ride it to the Shipwreck Islands
on a rising tide of stopped clocks, headless statues,
brass lamps, glass eyes, nautical maps,
candles burning underwater.
Where the debris ends, the water turns clear,
and the moon gently rocks you into sleep.
Sometimes the wind carries old voices asking
why you are neither married nor single,
why your documents say Missing Person,
and the face in your passport is gone.
It's just the gossip of parrots.
You live in perfect simplicity.
In storms, you anchor.
In the breeze, you sail.

THE DEFAULT JINGLE

I bought a cordless phone
made in China
When a call comes in,
it plays a tinny version
of "The Star-Spangled Banner."

Oh say can you see
By the dawn's early light

The default jingle announces
telemarketers, robot advertising,
medical billing, pollsters,
collection agencies, wrong numbers.

And the rockets' red glare
The bombs bursting in air

I hear America calling,
but I'm not picking up the phone.

A MERCHANT OF AMSTERDAM

On a fine Sunday in the seventeenth century,
a merchant in Amsterdam walks to church.
He sets a stately pace for the family.
If a servant girl giggles, she is shushed immediately.

The pastor clasps his hands, bows his head,
and prays for the safe return
of sailors from the sea.

The merchant thinks of the ships
that he has invested in.
They must be near Sumatra now.

He secretly finds the sermon unconvincing.
What's the use of heaven and hell?
People need to make good laws
and follow them. Right here on earth.

In the afternoon, he studies his accounts.
His wife buys too many fabrics.
The barrel-maker's invoice is illegible.
His tenants are behind again.

At twilight he goes to the window
to see if the night watchmen
are patrolling the canals
or still posing for Rembrandt.

SCRIBE OF THE TRIBE

I was the scribe of the tribe,
preserving the songs of our heroes.
One day the tribal leaders
called me into their sweat lodge.
The room was hot and crowded.
The Executive Chief spoke
through his happy-face mask.
"From now on," he said,
"anyone who wants to be a hero
must submit a Need for Quest form.
He must be fully insured.
If he slays a dragon or a monster.
 he must dispose of the carcass
according to department rules and regulations
Everyone should have a copy of those rules.
Does anybody *not* have a copy?"
I raised my hand. "How will this affect my scribal work?"
"We won't be using scribes anymore.
Hand in your ID card and get rid of that pile of
myths, legends, and fairy tales on your desk.
The bookkeeper wants your office."

STOPPING BY SLUMS
ON A SNOWY EVENING
With deepest apologies to Robert Frost

Whose slum this is I think I know.
His house is in the Hamptons, though.
He will not see me stopping here
to run in for a dime of blow.

The taxi driver yells and honks
and says he won't go to the Bronx.
The only sound is *shake, shake, shake
your booty* from the honky-tonks.

My smile is lovely, big and fake.
The cabbie tells me, "Beat it, Jake.
You'll get me busted by mistake
and I got other fares to take,
and miles to go before my break,
and miles to go, for Christ fuckin' sake."

JAFFA ROAD

On Memorial Day in Israel,
voices are lowered.
Dogs don't bark, flies don't buzz.
The only noise comes from an old café
that was torn down years ago.
The shadows gather here,
still reluctant to depart.
They fell on the old Jaffa Road
during an argument with History,
that tough scholar whose jaws can
crack armor and break bones.
An old shadow says, I used to think
that words carved in stone
were truer than words written in the sand.
Another one says, I remember hot black coffee,
how it poured from a small brass pot
and left a thick, bitter residue in the cup.
The newest one says, I'm just waiting
for all the shouting and shooting to stop.

CEREMONY FOR A NEW YEAR

The future says Hurry Up
The present says Slow Down
The past says Go Back

WANG WEI

The ancient Chinese poet Wang Wei
could capture the swiftest bird
with one or two marks on paper.

When he visited the mountains
in autumn, his calm voice
soothed the agitated horses.

If I close my eyes, I can see him,
an old man at a red and black lacquered desk,
writing poems without any words,
asking Heaven to have mercy
on the piper who steals a breath now and then
so that he can finish his song.

41

THE APOLOGY

After dinner with her parents, she went out
to find that statues of forgotten heroes
had surrounded her rental car
and were rocking it violently.
She said nothing and hurried past them.
The gates of the Old Town had been shut
but the *pop pop pop* of gunfire was clearly audible.
Puppets with broken strings huddled together.
Traffic lurched in a blare of horns.
Stone saints on the cathedral
turned their backs on the noisy multitude.
Down by the harbor,
a crowd knelt on the wet sand
and begged the drowned
to forgive them.

She started running.

THE JOURNEY

Lao Tzu went out to his garden
after a late summer storm.

Raindrops glistened on green leaves.
That explains everything, he thought.

DANCING WITH OFFICERS' WIVES

Under the linden trees, between the wars,
my grandfather took many a stroll.
He wore a gray fedora that he would doff
to officers' wives before asking them to dance.
He wore underpants that he would doff
to harlots in hotel rooms.
His skill at doffing won him many invitations.
He would sit in my grandmother's parlor
while she cut the lies out of newspapers,
trimming long articles to a sentence or two.
She lost her scissors when the city was shelled.
In fact, she lost everything. Eventually,
the foreign oppressors were driven out
and replaced by local oppressors.
We lived from potato to potato.
Strangers in ski masks set fire to our village
and urged us to discontinue our ethnic group.
We were so hungry and cold that winter,
we sold Grandfather down the river.
He doffed his hat to the police
when they came to arrest him.
With a twinkle in his eye, he said,
"I wish you all a speedy recovery
from the twentieth century."

CHANCE MEETING

Nobody knows who drew your self-portraits;
I guessed many times, but always guessed wrong.
I looked for you in streets now and then,
but I never thought I'd actually find you.
I do not know why random events
disguise themselves as the signs
of a clearly impossible fate,
but I am grateful for the misunderstanding.

THE WORLD AT NIGHT

The paranoid dreamer feigned sleep for hours,
hoping to catch a glimpse of the world at night.
He wondered if there was more out there
than just shadows and sideshows.
He finally slipped out of bed
and looked outside. He saw squat,
malevolent ogres climbing up the walls,

pausing only to tear out people's tongues.

Meanwhile, gangs of men in hard hats
were busy dismantling the sky.
Frightened, he locked all the doors and windows
and fell asleep. When he woke up,
he looked outside and saw
that the sky was reassembled,
people's tongues had grown back,
and the ogres were hiding

either in the house or under it.

CASUALTIES

The musicians played
till our ears fell off.
When morning arrived,
we were utterly shattered.
Steven stepped into the chicken yard
wearing a full-length bathrobe
like the Godfather,
like a prizefighter,
like Alexander the Great
counting the living casualties
to see if the battle had been won or lost.

A WOMAN GOT DRUNK IN BALTIMORE

and drove to her ex-boyfriend's house.
He wasn't home, but she had keys.
She entered and began to smash collected glass
and porcelain in a steady cold fury.
Then the ex-boyfriend walked in
with his new girlfriend. A quarrel erupted.
Unforgivable words were shouted face to face.
The guy threw both women out of his house.
The new ex-girlfriend took a taxi home
and called up her best friend, my wife,
and they discussed it for hours.
That was last night. This morning
my wife was too tired to do the laundry,
so now I'm stuck in a dim basement,
folding sheets and matching socks,
because a woman got drunk in Baltimore.

TRAGEDY OF THE PIG

The pig is not a stupid animal.
When he reaches a certain weight,
he will be slaughtered, smoked, and cured.
The pig knows this.
Has always known this.
Yet he can't stop gobbling down
whatever slop he's served,
because he is a pig.

NEWS OF THE WEAK

On Monday the king was dethroned
on Tuesday the country rejoiced
on Wednesday the dictator took charge
on Thursday his opponents vanished
on Friday he seized foreign assets
on Saturday no one would take his calls
on Sunday the army arrested him
on Monday the king was back on his throne

THE MUSIC OF MEMORY

I'm running toward the sound of opera
on the radio that my mother puts in
the kitchen window
while she hangs wet laundry in the yard.
Sheets billow on the line.
I smell bleach and damp grass,
but I don't see her anywhere.
Where did she go?
I am very worried.
The dead are absent-minded
and often forget the way home.

My mother sits at a big table.
"Do you want to draw?" she asks.
I nod and climb on a chair.
Wherever I move the crayon on paper,
the line follows. When I lift the crayon,
the line stops moving.
I want to ask why, but I know she won't answer.
The dead are not good
at explaining things to the living.

OUR CULTURAL HERITAGE

Every bright kid is an Einstein,
Mona Lisa's a pop singer's ballad,
Napoleon is a pastry,
And Caesar's an order of salad.

BIG CITY STORY

Late one afternoon in the last century
she approached me in a laundromat.
I was in Spin, she was in Dry.
I looked at her eyes, her lips, all her moving parts.
We chatted. She gave me her number,
but it was hard to reach her. She was rarely home.
I called at random intervals, let the phone ring
dozens, maybe hundreds, of times.
When I did catch her, we talked for hours.
Then she was unreachable again.
One day, answering machines appeared in stores.
I ran out and bought one for her.
When she saw it, she said, "I don't need
a machine to answer your question.
The answer is yes."

THE TENANT

Some years later,
I returned to my apartment,
found it totally trashed.
Empty bottles, half-eaten meals,
heaps of cigarette butts, obscene graffiti,
notices from collection agencies,
blood stains on the mattress.
But the party was over.
The tenant was gone.
He slipped away one night,
leaving my name on his unpaid bills.
and his face in my bathroom mirror.

AS I WAS READING

As I was reading *The New York Review of Books,*
a mouse appeared next my chair.
I held my breath,
slowly lifted the Review
and stunned the mouse with a mighty blow,
then another. I struck it repeatedly
with weighty critiques, dense prose,
and powerful arguments.
I wanted to kill that mouse
before it had time
to write a letter to the editor.

AGE OF SILENCE
For AKC and LH

My childhood belongs to a defunct age
Information was not a concept,
just a service provided by the phone company.
There was no media,
only a morning paper rolled up
and flung from a speeding bicycle
in the vicinity of your porch.

The nightly news opened with
a flourish of Beethoven.
The Sunday paper arrived with the funnies.
A letter with a six-cent stamp
could change your life.

At the end of the day, work stopped.
Lights out. Doors locked.
People went home to the same dinners,
the informal rituals of the table.

When the TV was off
and the kids tucked in bed,
the adults sat in armchairs,
knitting or smoking.

They lowered their empty thoughts
into a well of silence
and drew them up
brimming again.

WORDS FOR MY WIFE

Age dismantles me
inside and out,
yet it freely gives
what can't be bought
for any price.

The older I get,
the more time I've spent
with you.

FORGET IT

Forgetfulness is a sneak thief. You reach for a name, a face, a date. It's gone. *I've been robbed*, you cry out. But you don't own your thoughts any more than a bird owns its flight.

Learn to forget, sang Jim Morrison with husky conviction, washing his hands of the past until one day, in a bathtub in Paris, he forgot to keep breathing.

What did the past leave us? Only some postcards, porcelain dolls, Swiss Army knives, flasks, souvenir ashtrays, accordions, bird cages, a tailor's dummy, the keening of a ghost in the attic.

You were annoyed when your mother cleaned your room and threw out half your stuff without consulting you. The laws of forgetting make no distinction between good and bad clutter.

If you remembered everything you ever saw, heard, or felt, you would become incurably mad. Forgetfulness protects us but there is nothing tender about its mercies.

DANCER WALKING

I love to see a dancer walking
on ordinary ground, off-stage and off-duty
but graceful even pushing a grocer's cart.
The body becomes loose and light
when the mind isn't minding it.
The earth turns under the dancer's feet.
The moon and other satellites adjust their orbits.
At home the dancer dices
tomatoes and fries onions,
standing in the kitchen
like a heron paused between
sunset and the shore.

MY PLATFORM

I want to require every politician to spend one year
living like a broke, unemployed single parent.
I want soldiers, insurgents, rebels, guerrillas,
mercenaries, police officers, and gangsters
to recognize the futility of violence and stop fighting.
I want all the immigrant-blamers in America
to go back to the countries their families came from,
in small, leaky wooden ships.
I want to live without phone numbers, PIN numbers,
serial numbers, passwords, security codes,
deadlines, expiration dates.
I want to see the New York Yankees play
Manchester United.
I want to take Shakespeare to the movies.
I want poets to stop rearranging words and listen to life.
I want other things as well.
At the moment I am in no position to make demands,
but I am willing to negotiate.

THE CHILDREN OF DR. PARKINSON

At the brink of sleep I wake up
because I fear my own dreams.
Luminous numbers blink in the dark.
A minute can feel endless.
The random noises of the night startle me
Later, an exhausted dancing begins in my skull
My friends join me and the party starts.
We mumble, stumble, fall, drool,
freeze, stagger, shake and stall.
I'm afraid the spectacle is far from tasteful
You'd never guess that once we were graceful.

ECHO OF A SONG

Get on your sea-horse and ride
Gallop over the tide
Beneath the tumultuous surface
the sea is calm inside